# FINDING THE RESTING PLACE OF GOD

*Intercessory Prayer Handbook*

**DONITA GORDON**

FINDING THE RESTING PLACE OF GOD
Intercessory Prayer Handbook
All Rights Reserved.
Copyright © 2018 Donita Gordon

This book may not be reproduced, transmitted, or stored in whole or in part by any means, including graphic, electronic, or mechanical without the express written consent of the publisher except in the case of brief quotations embodied in critical articles and reviews.

All scriptures are taken from the KING JAMES VERSION (KJV): KING JAMES VERSION, public domain.

ISBN: 978-0-9997159-9-4

# DEDICATION

I dedicate this book to my mom,
Rev. Dr. Virginia F. Barnett
June 19, 1951- September 2, 2018

## *In Memory of Rev. Dr. Virginia F. Barnett*

## *A Kingdom Family Decree*

*"And if it seem evil unto you to serve the LORD, choose you this day whom ye will serve; whether the gods which your fathers served that were on the other side of the flood, or the gods of the Amorites, in whose land ye dwell: but as for me and my house, we will serve the LORD."*
Joshua 24:15 KJV

We will serve the Lord as a kingdom family. We will wake up in the mornings with Jesus on our mind and say a prayer thanking him for another day. We offer thanksgiving unto the Lord even during pain. We understand pain is inevitable when God is getting ready to promote you. We will purpose in our hearts to acknowledge the Lord and trust him to direct our paths. He will show us what clothes to wear, foods we should eat, and places we should go. Our home will be full of joy from the songs and the teachings we hear on the radio and tv shows. Our children will walk around the house with headphones not bopping to R&B but gospel.

They will sing, dance, and be happy in Jesus. We will sing and create songs while we clean, cook, and travel in the car.

Everything we do will be centered on Jesus because we are a kingdom family. We will watch Christian channels and movies. We will occasionally watch other movies but we are careful not to allow anything fearful or tormenting to enter into our spirits. We go to Worship Services, Sunday school, Bible Study, Prayer Meetings and Revivals. We pray for ourselves and intercede for others. We visit the sick, hospitals, jails, and nursing homes. We end our day the same way it starts, with prayer. Kingdom families are all about pleasing God and doing what glorifies the Lord. We choose to serve the Lord and we will serve the Lord as a kingdom Family.

Written By,

*Rev. Dr. Virginia F. Barnett*
*February 8, 2015*
*6:00 a.m.*

# TABLE OF CONTENTS

Dedication ............................................................... i

Kingdom Family Decree .............................................. ii

1. The Gap Generation ............................................ 1
2. Pray Without Ceasing .......................................... 7
3. Pressing Through The Dry Seasons .................. 15
4. Experiencing The Master's Touch Through Soaking Prayer ..................................... 24
5. Graced With Confidence .................................... 31
6. Going Deeper In Prayer ..................................... 37
7. Manifesting Your Destiny .................................. 48
8. Treading Into The Prophetic Streams During Prayer .......................................................... 59
9. Seize The Moment .............................................. 70
10. Soaking Prayer Guide ........................................ 78

## CHAPTER 1
# THE GAP GENERATION

How we interact with God through prayer has evolved over the past decades. The way our grandparents and parents prayed at home has quickly evaporated. Years ago, I can recall having family prayer every Saturday morning in my den. We were encouraged to get on our knees and tarry for the power of the Holy Ghost. My siblings and I would start off very sleepy and tired, but we quickly realized that the longer it took for us to call on the name of Jesus, the longer we would be on our knees. As early as the age of five years old, I can recall praying and hearing my siblings speaking in tongues. One of my sisters would be filled with the Holy Spirit and it could be compared to the sound of bumblebees buzzing around. That became an early indication for me that playtime was over and it was time to get serious about my time in prayer. My mom would anoint our heads with Holy oil and began to prophesy over our lives. That family tradition continued until our teen years when Saturday mornings were replaced with jobs and school events. As a mother of three, I wanted to carry out the family prayer tradition but was faced with the daunting challenges of attending sports, church events, and other non-traditional tasks that occupied my Saturday mornings.

Over five years ago, the Lord pressed in my spirit how important family prayer was. Yes, there was corporate prayer at church, but who was covering our homes with prayer? The enemy was waging war against our families and causing demonic activity to remain comfortable in our rooms. Many were neglecting to plead and cover their homes with the blood of Jesus. Not only were we avoiding training our children how to pray in the natural home, but we were also disregarding assembling in the spiritual home (church). The advancement of technology and streaming devices have changed how we worship and communicate with God. The great divide of how millennials develop relationships has changed. The absence of face-to-face encounters like Moses desired has created the birthing of the Gap Generation. The Gap Generation that was prophesied in the book of Ezekiel. *"And I sought for a man among them that should make up the hedge, and stand in the gap before me for the land, that I should not destroy it: but I found none"* (Ezekiel 22:30).

Gap insurance was invented as a policy to cover the total value of the car just in case the vehicle is completely lost during an accident. The car owner would not have to pay any out of pocket expenses when the car is damaged and the value has depreciated. When we stand in the GAP, we can ensure the blood of Jesus will cover what you are interceding for. You can stand in faith that you will have nothing lost, missing, or broken while you are standing in the Gap.

God is calling forth a chosen generation that will stand in the Gap for the next generation. Standing in the Gap often refers to filling the void or bridging the Gap until the next generation is capable of standing for themselves. This may mean the mantle cannot be passed down until there is ripe fruit being demonstrated in the individual's life. If the mantle is passed down prematurely, it can jeopardize the mission and vision. Therefore, a waiting or wailing period must take place to ensure the most-qualified individual is filling the position. Many who were considered to be the chosen generation back in the 1980-1990's have created a shift in the church which we see demonstrated today. They were able to break through the boundaries and walls of generational traditions. The moments such as Acts II and Azusa were experienced again back in Toronto, creating a new revival called the Toronto Experience.

God wants us to experience the same great revival by standing in the Gap through prayer. This revival can come in many forms. It can be in the form of fire as it was demonstrated with the prophet Jeremiah. Jeremiah described it as fire shut up in his bones. *"But his word was in mine heart as a burning fire shut up in my bones, and I was weary with forbearing, and I could not stay"* (Jeremiah 20:9). Ezekiel described revival as a breath of wind. God said, *"And I will lay sinews upon you, and will bring up flesh upon you, and cover you with skin, and put breath in you, and ye shall live; and ye shall know that I am the LORD"* (Ezekiel 37:6). Isaiah pronounced revival with a sound. *"And it shall come to pass in that day, that the great trumpet shall be blown, and they shall come which were ready to perish in the land of Assyria, and the outcasts in the land of Egypt, and shall worship the LORD in the holy mount at Jerusalem"* (Isaiah 27:13). One of the most noted forms of revival was demonstrated with the great pouring of the Holy Spirit. *"And it shall come to pass afterward, that I will pour out my spirit upon all flesh; and your sons and your daughters shall prophesy, your old men shall dream dreams, your young men shall see visions:"* (Joel 2:28).

We can look through the decades to see how God would pour out His spirit upon the generations, creating a revival upon the land. The common thread has always derived from a foundation of prayer. We are accountable for training up the next generation to ensure the pouring of the Holy Spirit, flame, sound, and wind of God are kept alive and moving through the generations, ensuring there are no generational gaps.

## *Meditate on this...*

1. Who do you feel compelled to pray for the most (yourself, family, church family etc...)?

2. Have you identified the successor in your family that will keep the flame of God burning?

## *Textual Approach:*

1. *"Be not ye afraid of them: remember the Lord, which is great and terrible, and fight for your brethren, your sons, and your daughters, your wives, and your houses"* (Nehemiah 4:14).

# CHAPTER 2
# PRAY WITHOUT CEASING

Over the years I have come to the knowledge of understanding that "My prayer time" with God is very important. Sometimes God calls us to seek Him early in the morning before the crack of dawn, other times He calls us to midday or midnight warfare prayer. The Father is more concerned about if we pray, rather than when and where we pray. There is an earnest desire for man to pray and have a relationship with Him. The Pharisees prayed aloud to be seen by others, but their communication with the Father was considered long-distance. Hannah's prayers were silent and nontraditional during her time, yet God answered her prayer.

Jesus knew the importance of prayer and believed it was one of the most essential weapons for fulfilling the ministry of the Gospel. Therefore, He gave special time to teach each of His disciples how to pray. Through experiences, I have noted the importance of shifting your time and location of prayer. This is due to a strategic warfare design. Once the enemy becomes aware of your battleground, he knows where to attack. As a warrior fighting the enemy through prayerful warfare, you must stay alert and a step ahead at all times.

Prayer was not always at the top of my daily "to do" list. Living a life filled with projects, deadlines, meetings, and family was considered the norm. As most busy adults, we try to balance our lives with prioritizing. So why wasn't prayer a priority in my life? I thought that by attending church and mid-week services I was fulfilling my obligations unto the Father. Somehow, with all the faithfulness to the church, I failed to be faithful in communicating with the most important person in my life. These challenges began to interfere with not only my professional life but also my spiritual life. I had a great desire to be available to God but I couldn't fit Him into my schedule the way I really wanted to. After waking up early for morning prayers, I would fall asleep within a matter of moments because I was tired. Do you know how it feels to make every attempt to reach church for intercessory prayer but somehow fall short?

Condemnation would often set in because I didn't feel as though I was praying enough. I had read spiritual books and heard testimonies about people praying for three to five hours a day. This made me question if I really had a relationship with God or if I was falling short over and over again. Yes, the enemy is a liar and a deceiver. Condemnation is a work of the flesh that the enemy uses to crush the spirit of believers. The Holy Spirit would remind me of His Holy Scripture.

> *"There is therefore now no condemnation to them which are in Christ Jesus, who walk after the flesh, but after the spirit"*
> **(Romans 8:1).**

Besides, I didn't want to make excuses for not communicating with my Father. Let's be honest, we live in such a busy world, with little time to rest or enjoy the presence of the Lord. The first thing I had to do was manage my time. This habit taught me early in life how to value relationships while achieving results. Time management (accountability of time) and self-management (accountability of behavior) have not always played a major role in my life. Frequently, I would use "I work better under pressure" as an excuse for my tardiness and last-minute behavior. It wasn't hard to have a desire to pray. It was the fitting it into my busy life that was hard to do. First, I had to acknowledge my behavior of living a prayer-less life. Secondly, I had to become accountable for the absence of time that I should've devoted to God. Learning how to value yourself and becoming a manger of one's self is the key. Once you decide to commit to God in prayer, you are capable of reaping a great harvest which God has appointed for your life.

With a made up mind and determined spirit, I began to set my cell phone alarms to remind me that it was time to talk to God. No matter where I was nor what I was doing, I acknowledged the alarm. It became my own personal *Clarion Call*. Jesus was calling me to a higher place of prayer. I began to pray in the car on the way to work and on the way home. I began to walk during my son's football practice, praying and communicating with

God. One day I went to visit my sister-in-law in North Carolina. While helping her move out of her apartment, I noticed she had a pile of blankets on the floor. She said, "It's my threshing floor where I meet God. The devil knows he can't touch me here in this space because it's been dedicated to God."

*"O my threshing, and the corn of my floor: that which I have heard of the LORD of hosts, the God of Israel, have I declared unto you"*
*(Isaiah 21:10).*

The book of Isaiah describes the threshing floor as a place where God separates the chaff (ungodly desires) from the wheat (godly desires). During prayer, it can best be described as a place where God grinds the sin away from your life as you surrender to the call of prayer. When you arise from your place of prayer, you leave the sinful nature on the ground. Prophet Isaiah was experiencing a time of penitence and mourning when God called him to surrender all. The sackcloth that he wore was considered a rough garment. God spoke to the prophet and told him to lay down the sackcloth and walk naked. The actions of the prophet Isaiah seemed foolish to those he walked with, but it was his obedience that mattered most. After God saw that he was obedient, he called him to the office of watchman. As a watchman, the prophet Isaiah was able to sit up high to ensure protection from approaching enemies. He was also capable of watching the movement of the enemy to warn against imminent danger. God is calling for the watchmen of this hour. He has required individuals who are devoted to the call to pray without ceasing.

After learning more about the threshing floor, I immediately went home and grabbed a pink towel from the closet. I anointed it with Holy oil and dedicated that space to God. For the first time in my prayer life, I was ready to lay myself down and pray. I was just like the prophet Isaiah, laying naked before him in the spirit. I wanted to empty myself and remove all forms of grief and guilt. Yes, there was grief from grieving the Holy Spirit when he called me to prayer and I did not answer.

> *"And grieve not the Holy Spirit of God, wherby ye are sealed unto the day of redemption"* **(Ephesians 4:30).**

The Holy Spirit was calling me to a higher place of prayer and I made excuses as to why I didn't obey. At first, it felt very strange laying prostrate (face down) on the ground praying. Praying longer than thirty minutes was new to me. Believe it or not, I felt closer to God on the floor. I spent time speaking to him and he spoke back to me. I had found "My Prayer Time" and I loved it. It was the place where I felt I had direct access to the ears of God. On a side note, my kids would open the door, looking for mommy but shut it just as fast because they couldn't see me on the floor. As time continued to progress, my *threshing floor* time began to increase. God began to give me visions, songs, and scriptures as I lay on the blanket. The best part was getting up off the floor feeling as though a ton of bricks had just been released from my back. The musical group Hillsong described my experience best when they wrote their hit song, "Touch the Sky."

> ***My heart beating, my soul breathing***
> ***I found my life when I laid it down***
> ***Upward falling, spirit soaring***
> ***I touch the sky when my knees hit the ground***

Upon completion of each chapter, there will be times of meditation used to stir up the desire to pray. The meditation questions are not to judge but to observe your actions, thinking, and praying patterns. The end result is for self-evaluation as we grow in the Lord and increase our desires to communicate with the Father.

## *Meditate on this...*

1. Where do you find yourself praying the most (car, church, prayer closet, etc...)?

2. How often do you hearken to the voice of God to pray (every day, occasionally, when you have setbacks, when you feel thankful when you are overwhelmed, during times of sorrow, when you are joyful, other)?

## *Textual Approach:*

1. *"Create in me a clean heart, O God; and renew a right spirit within me"* (Psalms 51:10).

# CHAPTER 3

# PRESSING THROUGH THE DRY SEASONS

During times of feeling defeated and wanting to quit, we often find ourselves experiencing a drought. It is at this time we are vulnerable to fall into the sin of omission (the result of *not* doing something God's Word teaches) or commission (sins that a person actively commits). We have failures and setbacks, which create a pit that we can't seem to escape from. We have now landed in a place where God's Glory has departed our life. The word *Ichabod* means literally "inglorious" or "there is no glory," and in her pain and despair, the woman (who is unnamed in Scripture) lamented over the loss of the Glory of God from Israel.

*"And she named the child Ichabod, saying, 'The glory is departed from Israel!' because*

*the ark of God was taken, and because of her father-in-law and her husband. And she said, 'The glory is departed from Israel, for the ark of God is taken"* **(1 Samuel 4:21–22).**

Through the years, I have discovered that you can participate in corporate worship in the house of God and neglect to spend individualized time in the presence of God. This lapse of God's presence produces dryness within our soul and begins to spill over into our spirit. The dryness we experience becomes a conduit and continues to travel into our families, ministries, finances, and workplaces. It is a terrible thing to experience a desolate place. Sometimes we are assigned dry seasons according to God's will and plan. It may not always come as a penalty for disobedience or rebellion.

As we develop a higher character in Christ, we are given assignments. Your assignment may be to a place, person, or geographic region. This is a place where God will determine what you are made of and what is within you. This dry season could be a place where your gifts will flourish to perfection or die. Often, what lies dormant could be raised to the highest level and compensate for the dryness that you are experiencing. God refuses to give us what we deserve because He loves us and has a great desire to preserve us.

There were many important people including God's great prophets who experienced dry seasons throughout the Bible. Mary and Joseph experienced a time of dryness and despair during the pregnancy of Jesus Christ. They believed that God would continue to direct their pathways and they trusted His will for their lives. They may have felt lonely and afraid with the feeling that the Glory of God had departed from their presence while in that trying season. The Glory of God was not only with them but also within Mary.

After the birthing of Jesus Christ, the Lord sent Wise men to seek them and refresh their spirits. What many have viewed as a natural outpouring of gifts, God viewed as a prophetic outpouring for the filling of His Glory into the Earth. Jesus was cleansed, prepared, and anointed to live a life where the presence of God could dwell permanently.

*"And when they were come into the house, they saw the young child with Mary his mother and fell down, and worshipped him, and when they had opened their treasures, they presented unto him gifts, gold, frankincense, and myrrh"* **(Matthew 2:11).**

The gifts that were given to Mary had great significance. The gold (Be cleansed) signifies the purification process, frankincense (Be prepared) signifies the perfumes and incenses that were set for prayer, and Myrrh (Be anointed) was a special oil used for anointing the body.

While in ministry, I have come to the realization that there are moments in your life in which you may experience great spiritual overflow, on the other hand, there are times in which you experience spiritual dryness. When you have what I call a dehydrated life encounter, your symptoms can include feelings of *prayer-less*, *worship-less*, and defeat. There's only one place you find yourself, and that's with an empty cup. In Luke 11:13, the Lord reminds us that our Heavenly Father will give the Holy Spirit to those who ask. God said that He would never leave you nor forsake you.

You somehow may have avoided the condemnation and judgment that you should have received from disobedience, but you must be reminded He is with you while you are experiencing your dry season. Here are three points which will increase your desire to be filled with the Holy Spirit.

1. ***Be Cleansed:*** *"Purge me with hyssop, and I shall be clean: wash me, and I shall be whiter than snow"* (Psalm 51:7).

2. ***Be Prepared:*** Change your garments and set an appointment with God. *"Wherefore seeing we also are compassed about with so great a cloud of witnesses, let us lay aside every weight, and the sin which doth so easily beset us, and let us run with patience the race that is set before us"* (Hebrews 12:1).

3. ***Be Anointed:*** Anoint yourself with Holy oil. You are now worthy to gain access because our confidence comes from God. *"You shall take the anointing oil and pour it on his head and anoint him"* (Exodus 29:7).

## *Believe and you shall receive*

You must believe that the Father will give you a fresh and powerful experience at His appointed time. Have the faith to believe that His Glory is accessible to you. Haggai 2:8-9 reminds us how the glory of the present house will be greater than the glory of the former house because the silver and gold belong to Him. God wants to fill you with His Glory.

In the book of 1 Samuel chapter 3, the boy Samuel lived during a time where the Word of the Lord was rare and prophetic visions were not widespread. Samuel was living during a *dry season*. As Samuel positioned himself in the tabernacle where the ark of God was located, he could hear the Father calling for him. Before God could cause a breakthrough to come forth, he wanted to know that Samuel would follow instructions. This encounter with the voice of God happened early in Samuels's life. In fact, it marked the beginning of his prophetic ministry. Samuel's spiritual advisor, Eli gave him very detailed instructions to follow. He told Samuel to do the following:

1. Go lie down

2. When he calls you – answer

3. Say, "Speak Lord, for your servant is listening."

Samuel and Eli (1 Samuel 3:1-9), knew the significance of the prostrate position in the temple. It was great for their faith to keep the lamp of the Lord's house shining throughout the night. The instructions that Eli gave Samuel can be used for soaking in the presence of God. When we lie down before the Father, it signifies a state of rest and surrender. We are surrendering our thoughts for his thoughts. We are laying all of our burdens down at the feet of Jesus. Once you position yourself in the Fathers presence, you can hear his voice. The Father will speak to your heart and deal with the matters of the heart. Scriptures tell us to enter his courts with a spirit of thanksgiving. In order to operate in true thanksgiving, we must reflect upon the issues of the heart. We must release the matters of anger, jealousy, and strife. Coming before the Father with pureness and clean hands will open our ears to hear what the spirit is saying. Lastly, we must clearly state that we want to hear and obey. *"Speak Lord"* (1 Samuel 3:4-7) denotes that you are listening. *"Your servant hears thee"* denotes I am your servant ready to obey your every command. It wasn't until

Samuel positioned himself in a place near the presence of God that he heard the Fathers voice. He opened his mouth, his heart and his spirit to be filled with the power of God. The Lord continued to reveal himself to Samuel. This revealing wasn't a once in a lifetime encounter for Samuel. Scriptures tell us that the Father continued to speak to him and revealed the plans he destined for his life. We too must chase after his beauty and the desire for a continuous encounter with the Savior. Once you have practiced the art of intercessory prayer you will be able to put yourself in a place of filling and pouring.

The Holy Spirit is your helper sent by the Father to assist you in your times of need. God's Holy Spirit was sent to dwell within you. He can help you overcome dryness and live a *prayer-ful, worship-ful,* and victorious life. He can help you to rightly divide the Scripture as he imparts his power into your life.

*"Likewise the Spirit also helpeth our infirmities: for we know not what we should pray for as we ought: but the Spirit itself maketh intercession for us with groanings which cannot be uttered"* **(Romans 8:26).**

## *Meditate on this…*

1. When was a time you experienced a dry season?
2. Did you feel compelled to reach out for prayer from a Pastor, prayer partner, church brother or sister, family member or friend?

## *Textual Approach:*

1. *"Redeeming the time, because the days are evil"* (Ephesians 5:16).

## CHAPTER 4

# EXPERIENCING THE MASTER'S TOUCH THROUGH SOAKING PRAYER

So often, I hear people say they can't seem to pray without having myriads of things pressing in on them. This is where the practice of soaking and resting in the presence of the Lord can help. Soaking up the presence of God can provide an anointed time of being with the Father. Soaking Prayers can be defined as the intimate time where you position yourself in a posture of rest in the Lord's presence. While in his presence, start to listen to anointed music that imparts your spirit, and bypass your mind.

This practice can be compared to an old Jewish tradition of *waiting on the Lord*. In earlier days, it was called "tarrying, slain in spirit, or lying prostrate" (face down) before the Lord. Despite what it is called, they all have a supernatural anointing from the Holy Spirit that often heals, delivers, rejuvenates, and allows individuals to be filled with the Spirit of the living God. As you linger in his presence, you are at a point of expecting God's renewal blessings to be poured back into your life.

To be "saturated" in God's presence, is to soak up His love rather than to have "exertion" in prayer. As you receive a touch from God, you begin to connect with the authenticity of the Holy Spirit's presence. You may often respond by resting or lying on the floor. God wants us to live a prayerful life filled with worship and an impartation of the Holy Spirit. He created us to *Barak* (to kneel down) and bless God as an act of adoration to the Lord. Chase after his beauty and be filled with His grace.

> *"O Come, let us worship and bow down, let us kneel before the Lord our Maker* **(Psalms 95:6)**

When the Master touches your spirit, it takes you from a mindset of work and performance and moves you to a new dimension of intimacy fueled by the profound need in our hearts to be closer to the Lord. It allows us to experience the Lord on a personal and intimate level. He confirms His Word over our life and commissions us to walk out our destiny on purpose.

And like the Spirit hovered over the deep, He will hover over us like the waters of the earth. His hovering presence prepares us to receive the seeds of life, love and destiny he wishes to plant in our lives. A lifestyle of prayer will transform moments of anxiousness and restlessness into lives of peace and trust.

> *"For to be carnally minded is death; but to be spiritually minded is life and peace"*
> **(Romans 8:6).**

The Holy Spirit will speak things to you during this time to be used in momentous ways. The revelations you inherit during this sacred time will enable you to overcome the dryness obtained through the trials of life. He will empower you with the fruits of the Spirit *(love, joy, peace, forbearance, kindness, goodness, faithfulness, gentleness, and self-control).* The fruits of the Spirit are simply God's way of enabling believers to do what he has called us to do through his divine powers and not our own strength. His power has given us everything we need for life as we are called by his Glory. Remember, it is the Holy Spirit which distributes the gifts of the spirit as he sees fit.

## *Moving into the Deep Calling…*

I can recall a time in which my daughter was two years old and she loved to lay beside me. She wasn't content laying under my arms. She wanted to climb and lay on my chest. As her mom, I wanted her to be comfortable, so I would place her underneath my arms. She would immediately cry to lay back on my chest. Once she was placed back on my chest, she would fall into a deep sleep.

The Holy Spirit quickened me and I was reminded that it's not enough to abide under the wings of the almighty but you must press into him. You must come to a place that you are resting directly on him. God wants you to experience the full immersion by being in his presence. My daughter positioned herself to achieve the best place not just for rest but security and comfort. You must position yourself to be filled with God's Glory. He can then begin to pour into the dry places of your life. You will then come to understand the principle of *"deep calling to deep."* The deeper you press into the presence of God, the more Glory he will pour into your empty vessel. Learn to live in the secret place of the deep calling. Live in the Glory of Jesus Christ by staying connected to his presence.

> ***"Deep calleth unto deep at the noise of thy waterspouts: all thy waves and thy billows are gone over me"*** **(Psalms 42:7).**

This place of deep calling is a place of God's excellence. Everything about it should reflect the beauty and excellence of the Lord. God's essence is experienced when you go into His deep presence. He will meet you there and allow His Glory to pass. God has called you by name and appointed you to go into the deepness of prayer.

Humble yourself by laying at the feet of Jesus. The cross, which represents our connection of the Father as the sacrificial lamb and our salvation, is both vertical and horizontal. As you descend into the deep he will allow you to ascend to the highest place of his will. You can go deeper and higher at the same time. You can go deeper, higher, and experience expansion when you have increased intimate moments with the Father.

There will be times the Father calls you to strictly lay before him and times of great impartation of the Father's heart and purpose. Prayerfully seek his will for your time to be healed and made whole. Don't delay your appointment with God any further. Take a moment for yourself right now to start your encounter with him. Finding the resting place of God will serve as a great outpouring. You will be consumed with the billows of his presence. This will enable you to serve more effectively in the body of Christ and build the Kingdom of God. Take a moment to meditate on the following Scriptures.

## *Scriptures on Resting*

*"The Lord is my shepherd; I shall not want. He maketh me to lie down in green pastures; He leadeth me beside the still waters. He restoreth my soul; he leadeth me in the paths of righteousness for his name's sake" (Psalm 23:1-3).*

*"Stand in awe, and sin not: commune with your own heart upon your bed, and be still. Selah"* (Psalm 4:4).

*"Rest in the Lord, and wait patiently for Him: fret not thyself because of him who prospereth in his way, because of the man who bringeth wicked devices to pass"* (Psalm 37:7).

*"Be still and know that I am God: I will be exalted among the heathen, I will be exalted in the earth"* (Psalm 46:10).

*"If ye abide in me, and my words abide in you, ye shall ask what ye will, and it shall be done unto you"* (John 15:7).

## *Meditate on this...*

1. What is an image that comes to your mind often during prayer?

2. Have you recognized the voice of God when you remain silent in prayer?

## *Textual Approach:*

1. *"After this manner therefore pray ye: Our Father which art in heaven, Hallowed be thy name"* (Matthew 6:9).

# CHAPTER 5
# GRACED WITH CONFIDENCE

There is a confidence that you can now enter boldly into the throne of God. The book of Hebrews states *"Let us therefore come boldly unto the throne of grace, that we may obtain mercy, and find grace to help in time of need"* (Hebrews 4:16). Pondering on past sins and afflictions make us feel unworthy to advance within the kingdom of God. The nature of sin itself produces an unhealthy state of guilt. The Prophet Isaiah said, *"Woe to me!"* (Isaiah 6:5-7). I cried. *"I am ruined!* For I am a man of unclean lips, and I live among a people of unclean lips, and my eyes have seen the King, the LORD Almighty." Immediately God dispatched his angels to go before Isaiah with a live coal. The angel touched his lips and spoke to Isaiah. *"See, this has touched your lips; your guilt is taken away and your sin atoned for."* Coal is a combustible black or dark brown rock found underground. You may be asking how something found in the dirtiest part of the Earth can be used for purification. Likewise, activated charcoal which is made from coal can be used to rid the body of unwanted substances. Many hospitals use charcoal as a detox for the body. The coal the angel used to purge the lips of Isaiah came from the Holy Altar of Fire. Our God is a consuming fire. He is a flame of fire that brings red-hot fiery revival to our lives. The angel dispatched with the live coal was a Seraphim. The Seraphim is the angel belonging to the highest order of angelic hierarchy and their name means burning one. These angels surround God's throne declaring his holiness night and day. The flames of fire are extracted from the Glory of God. The flames that surround the throne purify and change both the spiritual and physical desire of man. The prophet Isaiah had an encounter with the presence of God that marked the beginning of his ministry. This encounter allowed him to be purified with the coal so he could do the greater works the Father required of him. *"Who shall I send, and who shall go for us?"* and *the prophet answered, "Here I am, send me"* (Isaiah 6:8).

Queen Esther has also demonstrated the pattern for approaching the throne of a king with confidence. It was custom practice for a young lady to obtain a year's purification in order to approach the king. This purification process included six months with myrrh and six months with sweet spices. The myrrh was used for making the skin clean, smooth, and for giving the skin elasticity. Myrrh is a sticky, gummy substance that is used as a pain deadener. James Maloney describes it as a mixture of love and suffering, compassion and passion. The skin was saturated with spices to remove all of the bruises and scents from working in the field.

*" Now when every maid's turn was come to go in to king Ahasuerus, after that she had been twelve months, according to the manner of the women, (for so were the days of their purifications accomplished, to wit, six months with oil of myrrh, and six months with sweet odours, and with other things for the purifying of the women"* **(Esther 2:12 ).**

It wasn't until after a year of soaking the odors away that Esther was even considered worthy to grace the doorway of the king. Through promise and the favor of God, Esther was favored in the sight of the king. She gained entry into the intimate courts of the master.

> *"And it was so, when the king saw Esther the queen standing in the court, that she obtained favour in his sight: and the king held out to Esther the golden sceptre that was in his hand. So Esther drew near, and touched the top of the sceptre" (Esther 5: 2).*

Esther believed in the power of prayer and she walked through the courts with confidence. It was a divine appointment in which man denied access but God favored her. To approach the king and touch the scepter, was a breach of Persian etiquette and is punishable with death. This action is a demonstration of crying out to the savior for deliverance. This example of Esther can be compared to the act of approaching the Father and going deeper in the presence of God. It is the moment that God has granted you if we want to be accepted beyond the veil of His Glory. There are three notable actions to accessing the throne of God.

1. We must be Purified
2. We must prepare for the encounter
3. We must embrace the anointing

God wants us to be purified and come before his throne room with scents of pressed oil, myrrh, and spices. In the Hebrew, the word *mashach* means to rub or smear (with oil). God wants his presence to be smeared over us as a masterpiece. Purify yourself to enter into the prepared place. Absorbing God's presence is a time in which we simply come to be with our Father—no lists, no agendas, just resting in His arms of Love and laying at his feet.

In Exodus 33:18-23, Moses wanted to see the Glory of God but was denied access because Jesus had not yet gone to be with the Father. The ultimate sacrifice had not been paid to gain entry beyond the veils and into the Holy of Holies where the presence of God inhabits. Moses said, "I beseech thee, shew me thy glory" and God replied, *"I will make my goodness pass before thee. And he said, Thou canst not see my face: for there shall no man see me, and live."* Jesus went to hell and took the keys from Satan. He possessed the keys to the Kingdom and allowed all believers to gain access to the Glory of God that Moses so desperately wanted to experience. Through prayer and faith, we can approach God with freedom and confidence.

> *"In whom we have boldness and access with confidence by the faith of him"*
> **(Ephesians 3:12).**

## *Meditate on this...*

1. Have you identified what areas of your life God needs to purify before approaching God in prayer?
2. The next time you pray, leave the list and agenda, just worship God, remain silent, and journal how you feel.

## *Textual Approach:*

1. *"Watch and pray, that ye enter not into temptation: the spirit indeed is willing, but the flesh is weak"* (Matthew 26:41).

## CHAPTER 6
# GOING DEEPER IN PRAYER

You must believe that God will begin to pour his spirit into you and give you access to deeper waters even through your pain, trials, and tribulations. The book of John 4:4-26 teaches a lesson of Jesus and the Samaritan woman. While walking through Samaria, Jesus stopped by a well and saw Samaritan women. He asked the woman for a drink of water. The Samaritan woman said to him, *"You are a Jew and I am a Samaritan woman. How can you ask me for a drink?"* (For Jews did not associate with Samaritans.) Jesus answered her, *"If you knew the gift of God and who it is that asks you for a drink, you would have asked him and he would have given you living water."* Jesus answered, *"Everyone who drinks this water will be thirsty again, but whoever drinks the water I give them will never thirst."* Indeed, the water I give them will become in them a spring of water welling up to eternal life. The woman said to him, *"Sir, give me this water so that I won't get thirsty and have to keep coming here to draw water."* This woman initially lacked the confidence in her ability to draw from the well because of her identity.

Our destiny was planned while we were being shaped and formed in our mother's womb. We must continue to draw from the deep waters so we will never thirst again. The water Jesus gives is eternal life. As we draw from the well, we are able to share the water with others whom we may come in contact with. The Holy Spirit begins to pour into your spirit and creates an overflow anointing. Our unbelieving friends and family cannot draw from a dry well. We must keep our wells filled through the power of prayer and soaking in his presence.

If you really want to go deeper in prayer, add anointed worship music. Worship music always enhances your time with the Father and takes you into a deeper realm of prayer. Many believe the music must be soft and have no beat but the music you worship to can be varied according to your personality or culture. You should try various types of music and see which one ministers to your spirit. There are different genres of worship music and you can also mix it up. The ultimate goal is to go deeper in prayer with the intimate time you have designed.

John Belt likens the worship music encounter to "going into surgery, being put under anesthetic, and letting the Holy Spirit work in your heart like a surgeon would in an operating room." "It is a time of resting in such a way, just like being under anesthetic, and letting God, like the surgeon, have His way. We do nothing but submit to the process and trust God."

I can recall when I was going into labor with my daughter. I had an emergency cesarean due to the baby falling into a distressful position. The doctors and nurses began to panic and wanted me to be put under anesthetics immediately. I remember taking two breaths of oxygen, but when I awaken, my baby girl was already born. For eight hours I had no memory of the birthing process, the hurts, the pains, or the experience of holding my baby for the first minutes of her life. As awful of an experience that was, it can so easily be compared to the time we spend with the Father. We shouldn't be worrying about the pains of this life, the bills, or trials and tribulations.

This is the time God's presence will hover over you to reveal more of God's love, renew, repair, and saturate areas of life that are often left desolate or dry. As the believer soaks in God's presence, the Lord takes control and invites you into the Holy Place. You must have the faith that he has prepared a secret place and you have the authority to enter the resting place of God.

You must prepare your heart. Prepare your heart by confessing any hindrances or sin standing between you and the Lord. Give the enemy no place to come and accuse you during this time. Ask the Lord to search your heart and see if there be any wicked way in you (Psalms 139:23). Consciously separate yourself from the issues of life and surrender your physical, emotional and spiritual being to receive from the Lord. Ask Him to come and reveal His heart to you. Remember, there is no need to force anything or rush during this time. Just relax and wait on Him. There is no limit on how long you can stay or how often you soak other than your schedule. You can come to the well to draw as often as you wish. He is always where you are and He is always waiting. You can take a sponge and lay it in a bowl of water. Without touching the sponge, it will begin to absorb the water around it. Just like a sponge in need of water, allow Him to saturate you and experience an overflow.

## *Dreaming*

A disciplined lifestyle of intercessory prayer will often take care of the tendency to be so easily distracted by wandering thoughts. If you do get distracted and find your thoughts wondering during your prayer time, just stop and ask the Lord if He is trying to speak to you about the distraction or issue. If you feel He isn't dealing or ministering to you on the particular thought, just refocus on Him and don't be concerned. Again, it is not a time of working things up or making anything happen. It is a time of being filled and impartation.

We must have the faith to believe that even if we fall asleep he will still work in us. In Song of Songs chapter 5 verse 2 the Scripture says, "I sleep but my heart waketh." Therefore, if you go to sleep, you most likely need the rest. Just like the surgeon who continues to work on the individual who is fast asleep on the operating table, the Holy Spirit will continue to work on you. This is another reason it is important to create a comfortable environment that eliminates distractions.

Dreaming is a series of thoughts, images, and sensations occurring in a person's mind during sleep. The father has dreams and visions to impart while you rest in his presence. He wants us to pursue our dreams and passions. This can only come with a pure heart and gentle spirit. The dreams the Father imparts into your mind may not always make sense. We can learn from Joseph how God honors our ability to dream. One of my favorite books is Dream Giver: Following your God-given destiny by Bruce Wilkinson. This book denotes that each of us has a deep desire to know and fulfill our life dream. Many of us fail to live out this dream because of fear of the unknown and not believing that God can bring our dream to life. In The Dream Giver Wilkinson explains that our truest and deepest dream comes from God. God is the author of our dreams and our destiny is to bring Him the greatest glory.

Many times you can experience troubled dreams while resting in the presence of God. We should take the dreams as words of wisdom or word of knowledge. The dream is not to frustrate your purpose or cause fear. The closer you get to the Father, the greater concern he has for your life. He has your best interest at hand and wants us to be watchman standing on the wall. He wants to fill your life with the Word and allow you to be strong and courageous in the Lord. Joseph ministry of dreaming started at age seventeen. Through his inexperience and young age, his dream was misinterpreted by his family. Joseph waited a few years in order to see the manifestation of his dreams. He endured a lot of opposition and hardship but he persevered.

## *Experiencing Visions*

Prayer can also cause impressions, pictures, or visions to come to mind. Let your heart meditate on them and don't shut them down. The Lord is always faithful and worthy of being trusted to lead and guide you. Prayer enhances your ability to have visions. A Vision can be defined as a vivid apparition. If a sad memory comes to mind, don't run away from it, the Lord is most likely moving in your heart to heal any wounds associated with the memory. Just let go and if necessary audibly release the memory and or people to the Father.

There are many responses in the physical and spiritual makeup of people that may be revealed. Some common manifestations are weeping, joy, or the heaviness of the burden from intercession. The more you pray in His presence, the more encounters you will have. A few weeks ago, God gave me an impression of a forearm and the palm of a hand during prayer. I knew the impression was given to me by the Holy Spirit. What was it symbolizing? Just what was the Lord trying to speak to me about this forearm and palm of a hand? Once I became quiet before the Lord he spoke about the power to create. The Hebrew word Bara means to create. God wanted me to create what He wanted and not what I saw upon the Earth. Too often we look at what others are doing and try to imitate their vision. The forearm signified his strength. He said for us to look up into the hills from where our help comes from. All of our help and strength comes from God.

> *" Set your affection on things above, not on things on the earth"* **(Colossians 3:2).**

These types of impressions are common when you spend time in Prayer, so don't be afraid and trust Him to lead and guide you into all truth. All the mentioned experiences are valid and happen based upon the Fathers desires for your life. The most important thing to remember is the Holy Spirit is gentle. What He shares will be based on the Holy Scriptures to draw your focus to Him.

God imaginatively designed the brain. He wants to use the creativity for His Glory. The enemy has long sought to pervert the use of our imagination. There are greater things that God want to do in our life. Without a vision, we will perish. Our heart, mind, and eyes will be blinded.

While teaching science to a group of fourth graders, I begin to distinguish the three ways light is permitted to pass through. The first is opaque which is described as not transparent or translucent. It is impenetrable to light which means not allowing light to pass through. Next is translucent which allows a diffused or semi light to pass through. Finally, transparent permits the uninterrupted passage of light. Our encounters with God during prayer can be compared to the three ways light can pass through. *"Every good gift and every perfect gift is from above, and cometh down from the Father of lights, with whom is no variableness, neither shadow of turning"* (James1:17). When you have a life without prayer, the light of the father cannot pass through you to reach out to others (Opaque). Those who demonstrate a life with little prayer creates a little light to pass through (Translucent). A life with much prayer creates an uninterrupted ray of God's light to not only pass through you, but shine so others can view it (Transparent). The Holy Spirit will always draw you to his will and His Word so that his light can shine through you.

## *Meditate on this…*

1. Describe a time in which you went into deeper waters during prayer.

2. How would you describe your current prayer time with the Lord (Opaque, Translucent, or Transparent)?

## *Textual Approach:*

1. *"Ask, and it shall be given you; seek, and ye shall find; knock, and it shall be opened unto you:"* (Matthew 7:7)

# CHAPTER 7

# MANIFESTING YOUR DESTINY

God honors our obedience and our time of consecration that we establish during prayer. He rewards those who diligently seek him by revealing the mysteries of Christ. These mysteries are not hidden from you but you must gain access through the keys you obtain through prayer. It is important that you consciously choose your words. You must manifest your royal anointing to the blessings God has designed for you. Revisit your life when you didn't incorporate an appointed time of prayer. Take the time to consider carefully the course of your life. We must line up our words and continue to speak the blessings even when we do not see our prayers answered immediately.

*"Death and life are in the power of the tongue: and they that love it shall eat the fruit thereof"* **(Proverbs 18:21).**

While you are waiting on the promised destiny that God has called you to fulfill, it is important to maintain spiritual control. First, determine if the promised word God gave is a rhema word (download from the Holy Spirit) or logos word (found in the Scripture). God gives his children revelation but we must ensure that it is his will.

Maintain joy while you are waiting to distinguish his purpose and plan for your life. We should always pray, *"Thy kingdom come. Thy will be done in earth, as it is in heaven"* (Matthew 6:10). The promise that God gave you belongs to you and the devil cannot take it for you. God has a divine appointment for your life but you must remain faithful. Faithfulness means to be committed. You must be a faithful worker of the Lord through devotion and have a constant time of prayer. Don't allow fear to stop the manifestation of the blessings he has already promised.

## *Hidden Seeds*

When you think about a seed, it is first placed into the ground as lonely and dark. You must believe that your change will come even if you do not see the manifestation of your seed. A bulb is a seed that plant growth occurs from the basal or underground storage organs. A good example will be the onion, garlic, or tulip. Certain environmental conditions are needed to trigger the transition from one stage to the next, such as the shift from a cold winter to spring weather. One of the phases that a seed processes through is dormancy. A dormant seed is one that is unable to germinate in a specified period of time. Midlands State University (Mushayabasa, Tsvakai, 2018) described the various stages of dormancy. The natures of dormancy can also be compared to phases many Christians go through in the body of Christ.

- *Exogenous Dormancy*: a condition outside the seed which is considered to be a hard seed coat which water cannot pass through.

- **Endogenous dormancy:** seed has a condition within itself that prohibits growth.

- *Double dormancy*: seeds that require two years or two seasons to germinate.
- *Physiological dormancy*: seeds cannot grow or generate enough power to break through the seed coat due to physiological causes.
- *Combinational dormancy*: the seed that fails permission of water and cannot generate enough power to break through the seed coat due to physiological causes
- **Secondary dormancy**: after the seed has been dispersed and is ready to germinate an unripe or unfavorable condition stops the seed from growing.

I do not have a green thumb but I do know that an undeveloped seed is no different than a seed that was developed and couldn't grow. God has planted many seeds within the Body of Christ. The seeds are only watered through the time we spend praying and seeking the Lord in prayer. Somehow we expect the seed to work alone. We throw our seed into the ground and expect the seed to grow not realizing that it may be dying because it doesn't have enough water. If you are not seeing the fruit of your labor, you must ask God if your seed has gone into one of the dormant states.

We need to soak in the presence of God not only to fill our empty wells but to help water the seeds God imparts us with during prayer. Often we say that we are just waiting on the Lord. While waiting, you must continue to work and cultivate your seed. If you want to reap a harvest, there must be seeds that have germinated. Remember, the reward is based on faithfulness, not on the size of the responsibilities. Sometimes the smallest seed may have the greatest reward. If we are truly resting and waiting on the Lord, it will be a time of prayer and impartation.

David didn't have the ripest conditions when he was called as a king. He had to wait on the Lord and learned to seek out that intimate place within the house of the Lord. David's waiting was active as he sought to worship God and the beauty of his holiness. David also instructed Solomon how to wait on the Lord.

> *"And David said to Solomon his son, Be strong and of good courage, and do it: fear not, nor be dismayed: for the LORD God, even my God, will be with thee; he will not*

*fail thee, nor forsake thee, until thou hast finished all the work for the service of the house of the LORD"* **(1 Chronicles 28:20).**

## *Power of Potential*

Know who you are and what your true potential is. Potential is the amount of power lying within you. Many of us have not tapped into our full God-given potential. Every child of God has potential (Stored up energy). First, you have your natural potential. The natural potential is what God formed while we were shaped in our mother's belly. Your natural potential can be passed down from one generation to the next creating a family inheritance. Each person is born with their unique strengths and abilities that vary according to the gifting of God. The natural talent is neither a spiritual talent nor a gift of the Holy Spirit but it may be used by the working of the Holy Spirit.

> *"For the gifts and calling of God are without repentance"* **(Romans 11:29).**

The natural potential and gifts are irrevocable. Our natural potential is a display of the grace that God has given to man. We are not always deserving of the natural potential that God has given us. You can see the demonstration of the natural potential as evidence through basketball players, singers and politicians.

It is the spiritual potential that the believer receives at the time of their spiritual birth. This deposit of God given by the Holy Spirit may be described as the gifts of the Holy Spirit. The gifts of the Holy Spirit help you to fulfill your true spiritual potential.

The bible states there are different kinds of gifts. Every gift is given to believers by the same Spirit, which is the Holy Spirit. Each person must seek God for revelation on how to serve within their gifts. Every gift comes from God, however, there are different ways the Spirit works.

The gifts from the Holy Spirit include:

- To some people the Spirit gives a message of wisdom.
- To others the same Spirit gives a message of knowledge.
- To others the same Spirit gives faith.
- To others that one Spirit gives gifts of healing.

- To others he gives the power to do miracles.
- To others he gives the ability to prophesy.
- To others he gives the ability to tell the spirits apart.
- To others he gives the ability to speak in different kinds of languages they had not known before.
- And to still others he gives the ability to explain what was said in those languages.

*"Now there are diversities of gifts, but the same Spirit. And there are differences of administrations, but the same Lord. And there are diversities of operations, but it is the same God which worketh all in all. But the manifestation of the Spirit is given to every man to profit withal"* **(1 Corinthians 12: 4-7).**

Your potential is the source, virgin, or beginning of anything. Your potential starts in prayer. God wants you to maximize the potential he has given each individual. What a powerful giant you can be in the Gospel by combining your spiritual and natural potential. You may be pleased with where you are now but don't accept your present state in life as final. There is so much more God wants to release in your life. We need to allow God to breathe on us and cause us to move in the direction he wants us to go. There is so much work to be done for the kingdom but we must position ourselves before the Lord in prayer. Sometimes we need a gentle push to know that potential is lying within us. Queen Esther was nudged by Mordecai. *"For if thou altogether holdest thy peace at this time, then shall there enlargement and deliverance arise to the Jews from another place; but thou and thy father's house shall be destroyed: and who knoweth whether thou art come to the kingdom for such a time as this?"* (Esther 4:14). Esther's disobedience had the potential of causing her and her father's family to perish. There could have been a generational gap to receiving the inheritance. You must believe that the Father wants you to draw to prayer to obtain your royal position for such a time as this. Have a desire to be in the presence of God. Your desire for prayer should be so great that you crave enough to sacrifice for it. Sacrifice your Earthly desires for the Father's desires. Jesus made the ultimate sacrifice at the cross. Declare that you are a child of God with great potential to fulfill God's will.

There are three dimensions of manifesting your time of communication with the father. The three dimensions can be distinguished by its levels of characteristics.

1. ***Renew:*** Renew your passion for ministry (serving others). Stay focused on what God has called you to. Believe that God has given you a ministry that is catered to your personality, abilities, and knowledge. *"Not slothful in business; fervent in spirit; serving the Lord;" ( Romans 12:11)*

2. ***Create:*** Create what the Father wants and not what you see upon the Earth. Design a ministry that will last a lifetime. You may have a targeted audience but minister to the soul and spirit of man. *"Set your affection on things above, not on things on the earth" (Colossians 3:2).*

3. ***Expand:*** Our confidence to take a leap of faith is found within Christ. Don't be afraid to expand your vision. Impart your gifts into others and they will design a tailored ministry specific to their church needs. *"In whom we have boldness and access with confidence by the faith of him" (Ephesians 3:12).*

## *Meditate on this...*

1. Journal a time God gave you a gentle nudge by his Holy Spirit.

2. Where do you believe your hidden seeds are stored (wisdom, faith, miracles, healing, etc...?)

## *Textual Approach:*

1. *"And he prayed again, and the heaven gave rain, and the earth brought forth her fruit" (James 5:18).*

# CHAPTER 8

# TREADING INTO THE PROPHETIC STREAMS DURING PRAYER

The Word of God states *"Every place whereon the soles of your feet shall tread shall be yours: from the wilderness and Lebanon, from the river, the river Euphrates, even unto the uttermost sea shall your coast be"* (Deuteronomy 11:24).

During a time of great awakenings and prophetic activations, we have come to the understanding that God speaks to his people at various times and countless ways. During prayer, we must allow the love and affections we show to the Father to move through deeper waters. Prayer leads us to the river of the prophetic. God uses his vessels through a variety of prophetic streams. A few can be classified as the following:

- Writing
- Declarations and Decrees
- Psalms
- Movement

> ***"God, who at sundry times and in divers manners spake in time past unto the fathers by the prophets,"*** **(Hebrews 1:1)**

As God begins to press into the hearts and minds of his people, we often look to what we have heard, seen, or observed to understand what God is trying to reveal. God instructs his people to remember his precepts, recount his mighty works, and recall the vision and dreams He has impressed upon us. There is an appreciation for what the Fathers and prophets have allowed us to learn. Is it possible that God can also be calling you to create what you have not seen or heard? Is it possible that God is calling you to speak and declare what has not been observed? God is calling us to tread into deeper waters. Dare yourself to prophesy (foretell the Word of the Lord)!

Look unto the heavens to create the impressions of the Holy Spirit. We are living during a time of social media, videos, and recordings. It is imperative that we look to the heavens for clarity. How do you create what you believe and do not see? What is seen emerges from the secret place in prayer. The only way to release the anointing in a greater magnitude is to lay before the Lord in the secret place. Our worship to the Father produces a pressing of the olive. In return, the Father will extract the oil from the pressing to produce a greater anointing over your life. You should expect to experience a great manifestation of the kingdom of heaven when it occupies Earth through the power of prayer.

> ***"Thy kingdom come. Thy will be done in earth, as it is in heaven"* (Matthew 6:10).**

One of the streams that will be released during prayer is journaling or writing. Prophetic Writings are the revelations that God give you to foretell the gospel under the inspiration of the Holy Spirit. The book of revelations speaks of how God revealed his plans by sending his angels to his servant John. He was able to visually see God's Words about prophecy and was ordained to write what he saw. *"I am Alpha and Omega, the first and the last: and,*

*What thou seest, write in a book, and send it unto the seven churches which are in Asia; unto Ephesus, and unto Smyrna, and unto Pergamos, and unto Thyatira, and unto Sardis, and unto Philadelphia, and unto Laodicea"* (Revelations 1:11). The seven churches represent the seven continents of the world. During your writings, there will be times that you are mandated by God to write what is pertinent to the seven continents of the world. You must write, therefore, what you have seen, what is now and what will take place later.

The prophet Isaiah was a great example of a prophetic writer. He often wrote about the prophetic burdens he was imposed with to bring God's judgment. As Jesus was handed the book of the prophet Isaiah, He opened it. He searched the place where it was written: *"And there was delivered unto him the book of the prophet Esaias. And when he had opened the book, he found the place where it was written, The Spirit of the Lord is upon me, because he hath anointed me to preach the gospel to the poor; he hath sent me to heal the brokenhearted, to preach deliverance to the captives, and recovering of sight to the blind, to set at liberty them that are bruised, to preach the acceptable year of the Lord"* (Luke 4:17-19).

His writings were so important that Jesus quoted the writings while being tempted in the wilderness. *"It was also written "man shall not live by bread alone"* (Luke 4:4). This Scripture signifies the importance of writing it out.

Journal writings are an introduction to writing prophetically. Often it is not enough just to pray and go, especially if the Lord has spoken something to your heart. Throughout the journaling process, you may begin to see a theme or trend of how the father speaks to you. Seek the Father, as to how you should proceed with the journal writings. He may be pressing you to intercede (pray), obtain spiritual discernment (having the insight of God), or revealing words of knowledge (what is unknown). He could also have a bigger plan for your journal writings that have not been revealed for this season. God could very well use your journal writings for published writings or turning them into decrees. Most importantly, the Father could just want to communicate with you.

The second stream God will lead us to tread in is through the power of decreeing, declaring, and affirming. A declaration or decree can be best defined as the *Logos Word* (written Word of God) or a *Rhema Word* (God's spoken Word). Transcribe the words that he has written on the tablet of your heart and the visions you see into decrees. The things He gives you are meant to edify and build the body of Christ. After journaling or scribing what the Father has imparted upon your heart, record the words into first person, thereby turning your words into affirmations. Take your declaration and speak it back over your own heart and spirit. Speak it back over your life and family.

Speak in agreement with Him according to Deuteronomy 28: 2-13. This Scripture denotes the blessings God has already chosen for your life with obedience. God has already promised to be your Lord and grant you the Promised Land. He still demands diligent obedience in order to receive all the rich blessings you are decreeing upon the Earth.

Consider each declaration or decree like a medicine meant to preserve and transform your life. The decrees you speak are to cause you to grow, produce perseverance, and allow you to walk in freedom. They cause you to be fruitful and multiply. Like talents, they should not be buried, but multiplied through the agreement of the spoken word. The more you speak the more you will believe and become obedient to His call on your life. The words and revelations He gives you are for rooting out, pulling down...they are to destroy and overthrow the plans of the enemy and finally to build and plant according to Scriptural text. *"Then the LORD put forth his hand, and touched my mouth. And the LORD said unto me, Behold, I have put my words in thy mouth. See, I have this day set thee over the nations and over the kingdoms, to root out, and to pull down, and to destroy, and to throw down, to build, and to plant"* (Jeremiah 1:9-10).

God not only impress images, words, and decrees, but he also speaks through the psalms. By definition, a psalmist is one who writes, composes, or plays sacred music. It can be scheduled or spontaneous. The Psalms command us to sing a new song to God to make room for fellowship and usher us deeper into His presence.

As we learn to focus our spontaneous expression of songs on Jesus during prayer, we begin to tread into deeper waters. This intimate form of psalms allows believers to become more engaged with the communication exchanging before us. Connection and communication should be taking place during prayer if you want to experience a mighty move in the prophetic realm.

> *"Sing unto him a new song; play skillfully with a loud noise"* **(Psalms 33:3).**

God is giving us a Word and is communicating to us through his spirit in prayer. We must remember we are simply tools being used to communicate the message of God. True praise and worship come from the inner man. Here is where the Glory of God is birthed in us. The Father starts manifesting his Glorious presence, allowing communion to take place. In him do we live, move, and have our being! We begin to see ourselves as desperate deer panting for streams of water.

> *"As the hart panteth after the water brooks, so panteth my soul after thee, O God"* **(Psalm 42:1).**

The last stream we will focus on is movement. We have read in previous chapters about the importance of resting and lying prostrate before the Lord, however, movement is also a significant part of prayer. During prayer many will see signs, wonders, and miracles (2 Cor. 12:12) due to the shift that comes from our movement. We can see God ministering through the movement and use of worship tools. Do we not speak with our bodies through the language of movement? We can tell a story with our bodies even if there is no music at all. As Spirit-filled believers, our bodies can speak divinely inspired utterances. We can call those things into existence that be not as though they were.

## *The Key is to Linger in His Presence*

True prayer comes from the inner man. Here is where the Glory of God is birthed in us and he starts manifesting his Glorious presence. This is when communion takes place between you and the Father. In him do we live, move, and have our being! We begin to see ourselves as we truly are, in need of him, and how gloriously wonderful he is. The revelations He gives you will permit you to release superficial selfish gains you might have for His Glory. Praying with a Purpose takes advantage of every Word God speaks.

Don't be afraid to go into the deep waters. Press into Jesus! In Luke 11:13, the Lord tells us to press in to receive that our heavenly Father will give the Holy Spirit to those to ask. This is what the Bible says: *"The Lord is my shepherd; I shall not want. He makes me to lie down in green pastures; He leads me beside the still waters. He restores my soul" (Psalm 23:1-3).*

Love should be the number one desire when seeking to linger in the presence of God. We should love God so much that we want to spend time with him. Our love for the Father should motivate us to say yes to God in prayer. 1 Corinthians 13:2 says it so plainly, without charity (love) we are nothing. Even if we pray powerfully for hours if we do it without love it is all in vain.

> ***"And though I have the gift of prophecy, and understand all mysteries, and all knowledge; and though I have all faith, so that I could remove mountains, and have not charity, I am nothing" (1 Corinthians 13:2).***

## *Meditate on this…*

1. After prayer, which prophetic stream helps you to linger in the presence of God (writing, singing, declarations, affirmations, etc...?)

2. Write affirmations down in your journal that express how much God loves you and in return how much love you have for him.

## *Textual Approach:*

1. *"Again he said unto me, Prophesy upon these bones, and say unto them, O ye dry bones, hear the word of the LORD"* (Ezekiel 37:4).

2. *"I have called upon thee, for thou wilt hear me, O God: incline thine ear unto me,* and hear *my speech"* (Psalms 17:6).

## CHAPTER 9

# SEIZE THE MOMENT

Seize the day that you have decided to set that appointment with a sense of anticipation. Take any opportunity to cease striving to make things happen and enter his rest. You will be amazed how the changes on the inside display themselves on the outside and to the world around you.

> *"But thou, when thou prayest, enter into thy closet, and when thou hast shut thy door, pray to thy Father which is in secret; and thy Father which seeth in secret shall reward thee openly"* **(Matthew 6:6).**

Finding the resting place of God will not come through your own power or knowledge. It will take the supernatural wisdom of God to tap into this realm of the spirit. As noted at the beginning of the book, you must be intentional. Start off with balancing yourself, family, church and business affairs. Maintain healthy relationships with the people who matter most to you. Prayer is building a relationship with God. Remember, he desires to have healthy relationships with his children. Revelation 12:12 states, *"Devil's time is short"* and we are living in the last days. As Satan's work has become more intense our prayers must become more effectual.

> ***"Confess your faults one to another, and pray one for another, that ye may be healed. The effectual fervent prayer of righteous man availeth much"*** **(James 5:16).**

There are 60 seconds in a minute, 60 minutes in an hour, 24 hours in a day, 7 days in a week, 4 weeks in a month, 12 months in a year, 10 years, in a decade, 10 decades in a century, and 10 centuries in a millennium. Use your time wisely while you are upon the earth. Make every minute count. The Apostle Paul tells us that we are in a spiritual battle and there is no time for indecision. The war is against your offspring. It is declared upon the remnant of the seed as identified in Revelations 12:17.

The ability to control your habits, thoughts, and behavior will produce a disciplined life. Self-discipline will be the bridge to close the generational gaps. You must be persistent about your time devoted to prayer. Don't give up when you fall back into old patterns. Follow the pathway to having a disciplined prayer life using Matthew 6:9-34 approach.

- Offer Thanksgiving
- Ask for Forgiveness
- Meditate on his love
- Listen for him to speak and journal the responses
- Maintain a spiritual diet eating the scroll (bible)
- Rest in his presence
- Spiritually Exercise to become strong in your faith
- Organization is Key
- Persistence carries you a long way

*"Even so faith, if it hath not works, is dead, being alone"* **(James 2:17).**

Planning for tomorrow is time well spent but worrying about why you didn't pray is wasted time. Carefully planning ahead about your prayer goals, prayer targets, and prayer schedules will alleviate most of your worries about prayer. Don't allow your plans to interfere with your relationship you have built with God.

Richard Foster tells the story of an elderly lady who had been working at prayer with her own strength but without ever sensing God's presence. Her archbishop encouraged the lady to go to her room each day and "for fifteen minutes knit down before the face of God, but I forbid you to say one word of prayer. You just knit and try to enjoy the peace of your room."

The lady received his counsel but thought, "Oh, how nice. I have fifteen minutes during which I can do nothing without being guilty!" When she began to enter the silence created by her knitting, she stated "I perceived that this silence was not simply an absence of noise, but that the silence had substance. It was not the absence of something but the presence of something." As she continued her daily knitting, she discovered that "at the heart of silence there was He who is all stillness, all peace, all poise." The lady had let go of her striving efforts to enter the presence of God. By letting go, she discovered God's presence was already there.

Richard Foster goes on to state, "Resting in God does not mean resignation or idleness. It does not mean that we sit back and hope God will do something. Rest is what is called "recollection". Recollection means focus. It means tranquility of mind, heart, and spirit."

Praying is an adventure that takes one deep into the realms of God's presence. A place where two minds, two hearts, and two voices can communion. You must believe that today is the day and this is the moment that Jesus is inviting you into his inner courts.

> *"There remaineth therefore a rest to the people of God. For he that entered into his rest, he also hath ceased from his own works, as God did from his own works"* **(Hebrew 4:9-10).**

Experience God in his majesty just like Ezekiel. Dance in the presence of the King like David. See the train of the Lord filling the temple like Isaiah.

He will show you his glorious presence just like Moses. This is the time to see the glorious splendor of the Lord.

### *Prophetic Decree December 12, 2013 6:33 p.m.*

The seers shall be awakened with a trumpet sound. The trumpet will blow. The ear shall awaken. The ears have eyes in the deep canal of the ear. The ear shall be seers. The ears will serve a function to see. Scales shall be removed from the eyes of seers. Eyes shall have the function to see and hear and the mouth shall awaken and declare what thus saith the Lord. The mouth shall speak what God says and sees. Those things that are not pleasing to the Lord, the mouth will hear, see, smell, taste, and feel as senses are being awakened and many will hear the voice of God like never before.

Many shall see signs and wonders in a greater way. A great awakening is happening. Many shall return to Christ to find the Lord and the dead in Christ shall awaken. There are many seers with scales on their eyes. Scales will be removed and they shall see the salvation of the Lord with heightened senses. They shall have hindsight as senses are being reactivated and awakened. They shall have greater foresight and a panoramic vision to see all around in the great awakening.

> *"For this people's heart is waxed gross, and their ears are dull of hearing, and their eyes they have closed; lest at any time they should see with their eyes, and hear with their ears, and should understand with their heart, and should be converted, and I should heal them."*
> **(Matthew 13:15)**

## *Meditate on this...*

1. "Stand in awe, and sin not: commune with your own heart upon your bed, and be still. Selah" (*Psalm 4:4*). Ask God to show you His Glory.

2. "Rest in the Lord, and wait patiently for Him" (Psalm *37:7*). Patiently wait for His Glory to be revealed. Write what you experience.

## *Textual Approach:*

1. *"After two days will he revive us: in the third day he will raise us up, and we shall live in his sight"* (Hosea 6:2).

2. *"I exhort therefore, that, first of all, supplications, prayers, intercessions,* and *giving of thanks, be made for all men"* (1 Timothy 2:1).

# CHAPTER 10

# SOAKING PRAYER GUIDE

The purpose of the soaking prayer Guide is to teach participants how to enter a process of self-examination and purification by the Holy Spirit.

The following Guide is given as a general pattern: it is understood that each individual is free to follow the leading of the Holy Spirit, as he or she may be led into the presence of God.

## **You Will Need the Following Items:**

1. Your Bible
2. Paper and pen or pencil for journaling.
3. This Soaking Guide
4. Worship Music and/or worship tools
5. Prayer Shawl or towel for resting

*Keyword Dictionary Definitions*

**Soak:** To become thoroughly saturated by immersion

**Lie down:** To place oneself, or be in a prostrate position in order to rest.

**Quiet:** To be untroubled, free from activities or distractions. Still, calm.

**Rest:** To relax from exertion, or labor, to repose or sleep, a pause or interval.

**Wait**: To stay in one place, or remain inactive in expectation of something.

**Listen:** to concentrate on hearing something take heed, pay attention

## The Soaking Structure:

1. Each individual should find a private place of prayer: in the bedroom, garden, den, special chair, etc. Remain in quietness as you enter your place of prayer. You are free to stand, lay, kneel, or walk during this time of quietness.

2. Spend as much time as you can worshiping the Father. Calling on the wonderful names

of God and offering praises and thanksgiving to God. Enter His presence and begin to focus on that presence, giving yourself over to the appointment that you have set with God.

## *Opening Prayer*

*God, we hallow your name, you are holy,
you are merciful,*

*Your kingdom come into my presence, your will be done during this time, make yourself known to me in this time of solitude.*

*Forgive and cleanse from my life those sins and distractions that prevent me from being attentive and faithful to you. I forgive others who have trespassed against me. Grant me beauty for ashes, the oil of joy for mourning and the garment of praise for the spirit of heaviness. Anoint me and impart faith, wisdom, and courage to see and rejoice in your promises for my life.
Amen.*

## *Ten Prayer Targets*

1. Quicken me to hear my heavenly father's voice and lead me to a time of emptying out my imperfections and filling me with your presence.

2. Extend a hand of protection against evil thoughts, mirages, or plans that Satan may have spiritually or physically positioned against me.

4. I intercede in faith, believing that my life will serve as a vessel for you to fill me up with your Holy Spirit so those I come in contact with will have the opportunity to make Jesus their Lord.

5. I believe the Lord of the harvest will thrust me as a perfect laborer to share the good news of the Gospel.

6. I call debts of sin paid in full, canceled, or dissolved. God will send forth anointed individuals that will sow spiritually into my life.

7. I pray that the mission and vision will be fulfilled in its rightful time and season.

I proclaim that the atmosphere of the surrounding area be filled with the presence of God.

8. I receive favor, divine health, wellness on spirit,

mind, will, and emotions as I fulfill my appointment with God.

9. Heavenly Father open the gates of Heaven above me for provision, Deliverance, wisdom, protection, and healing right now as I prevail for the outpouring of the Holy Spirit.

10. I claim that I have been granting access to the throne room and granted victory through the power and blood of Jesus Christ.

## *SILENT worship through the playing of instrumental Songs*

Don't be in a rush to enter his Glory. Wait and allow his presence to lift you up into glory. As thoughts that are restless arise, give them to the Lord, letting them go, rather than holding on to them. Offer God all the stresses and concerns of your life. Surrender yourself over to God.

*"But they that wait upon the Lord shall renew their strength; they shall mount up with wings as eagles; they shall run, and not be weary; and they shall walk, and not faint."* **(Isaiah 40:31)**

## *Scripture Readings Guide*

What are these Scriptures saying to you today?

How does each passage offer personal application for your life?

## *Journaling*

Write down some of your innermost thoughts, imprints, and emotions you may be experiencing during this time of saturation.

- What is your will for my spiritual life?
- What changes in my daily life are you calling me to make at this time?
- What do I need to devote more and less attention to?

## *Declarations and Decrees*

- The LORD your God will set me high above all the nations on earth.
- I will be blessed in the city and blessed in the country.
- The fruit of my womb will be blessed, and the crops of my land and the young of my livestock

- My basket and my kneading trough will be blessed.
- I will be blessed when I come in and blessed when I go out.
- The LORD will grant that the enemies who rise up against me will be defeated before me. They will come at me from one direction but flee from me in seven.
- The LORD will send a blessing on my barns and on everything I put my hand to. The LORD my God will bless me in the land he is giving me.
- The LORD will establish me as his holy people, as he promised me on oath, if I keep the commands of the LORD my God and walk in obedience to him. Then all the peoples on earth will see that I am called by the name of the LORD, and they will fear you.
- The LORD will grant me abundant prosperity
- The LORD will open the heavens, the storehouse of his bounty, to send rain on my land in season and to bless all the work of my hands.

- I will lend to many nations but will borrow from none.
- The LORD will make me the head, not the tail.
- I will always be at the top, never at the bottom
- In the name of Jesus, I declare the promises of God, which are yea and amen
- I declare the Holy Spirit will make me healthy and strong in spirit, soul, and body
- I decree that my eyes are developing to see and my ears are developing to hear in the spirit realm.
- I will give you every place where you set your foot, as I promised Moses
- I declare that your mind will be strong and disciplined in the faith
- I decree the oil of God will be poured into my dry areas
- I declare that prayer and worship will flow from my spirit to the very throne room of God

- We receive revival, renewal, restoration, and a refill of your power
- I declare your kingdom come and will be established in my life

## *Closing Prayer*

Lord, as I am lead to this time of closing thank you for meeting me with your love. I declare that the Holy Spirit has opened up all past hurts and healed me. Allow me to grow in freedom. I want to stay full of the Holy Spirit until you require me to pour it out through intercession for my family, friends, the body of Christ, and sharing of your Gospel to the world. I want to continue the pattern of taking time for soaking in God's presence and experiencing an overflow so I may testify to what God is doing in my life.

## *Scripture References*

***Psalms 23:1-3*** – *"The LORD is my shepherd; I shall not want. He maketh me to lie down in green pastures, he leadeth me beside the still waters. He restoreth my soul. He leadeth me in the paths of righteousness for his name's sake …"*

***Psalms 131:2*** *– "Surely I have behaved and quieted myself, as a child that is weaned of his mother: my soul is even as a weaned child."*

***Psalms 4:4*** *– "Stand in awe, and sin not: commune with your own heart upon your bed, and be still. Selah."*

***Psalms 37:7*** *Rest in the Lord, and wait patiently for him: fret not thyself because of him who prospereth in his way, because of the man who bringeth wicked devices to pass…"*

***Matthew 11:28-30*** *-" Come unto me, all ye that labour and are heavy laden, and I will give you rest. Take my yoke upon you, and, earn of me; for I am meek and lowly in heart; and ye shall find rest unto your souls. For my yoke is easy, and my burden is light"*

There are several other Scriptures you might want to look up, including:

***Hebrews 4:9-11; Isaiah 40:29-31; Psalm 27:14; Proverbs 1:33; Luke 10:39 and Hosea 2:14.***

## *Prayer and Worship Instruments*

There are various prayer and worship instruments that will escort you right into the courts of the throne of God. The following tools will give you a brief definition and Scriptural reference.

*Tallit* - the Tallit is a prayer shawl with specially knotted fringes, called tzitzit. The tallit is a movable tent which symbols going into our prayer closet. *"Speak unto the children of Israel, and bid them that they make them fringes in the borders of their garments throughout their generations, and that they put upon the fringe of the borders a ribband of blue:"* (Numbers 15:38)

**Prayer cloth** – prayer cloths are small pieces of fabric used for faith healing in some Christian denominations. Their usage originates in the book of Acts 19:11-12, *"Which Paul the Apostle touched scraps of fabric, which were then used to heal the sick."*

**Worship Flags/Banners** – colorful banners, flags and streamers are used as powerful signals against the enemy. *"And he shall set up an ensign for the nations, and shall assemble the outcasts of Israel, and gather together the dispersed of Judah from the four corners of the earth"* (Isaiah 11:12).

**Billow cloth** - a billow cloth is yards of fabric that is used to create waves of glory. It can cause a shift in the atmosphere in prepare you for God's presence. *"Deep calleth unto deep at the noise of thy waterspouts: all thy waves and thy billows are gone over me"* (Psalm 42:7).

**Shofar** - a shofar is an instrument made from the horn of a ram. *"Blow ye the trumpet in Zion; and sound an alarm in my holy mountain. Let all the inhabitants of the land tremble, for the day of the LORD cometh, for it is nigh at hand"* (Joel 2:1).

**Mattah -** or prayer stick, or prayer staff, or prayer rod, is made of high-quality materials. All the scarves are tailored with feathers or stones.

## *Textual Approach*

*"And Miriam the prophetess, the sister of Aaron, took a timbrel in her hand; and all the women went out after her with timbrels and with dances." (Exodus 15:20) -* **Worship tool of choice was her tambourine.**

*"And David danced before the LORD with all his might; and David was girded with a linen ephod" (2 Samuel 6:14). -* **Worship tool of choice was his linen ephod or garments**

*"O come, let us worship and bow down: let us kneel before the LORD our maker" (Psalms 95:6). -* **Worship tool of choice was body as an instrument.**

*"Let the high praises of God be in their mouth, and a twoedged sword in their hand;" (Psalms 149:6) -* **Worship tool of choice were swords**

*"We will rejoice in thy salvation, and in the name of our God we will set up our banners: the LORD fulfil all thy petitions" (Psalm 20:5).* - **Worship tool of choice banners/ flags.**

*"But lift thou up thy rod, and stretch out thine hand over the sea, and divide it: and the children of Israel shall go on dry ground through the midst of the sea"* (Exodus 14:16). - **Worship tool of choice was a rod/ Mattah.**

# REFERENCES AND RECOMMENDED READINGS

- The Bible (*King James Version*).

- Goll, Jim. *The Lost Art of Intercession Expanded Edition: Restoring the Power and the Passion of the Watch of the Lord.* Shippensburg, PA: Destiny Image, 2007. ISBN: 978-0-7684-2428-7.

- Mitchum, Dean 2012, Prophetic Worship 101: Understanding the Ministry of Prophetic Worship

- Pierson, Mark 2010, The Art of Curating Worship: Reshaping the Role of the Worship Leader.

- Foster, Richard J. *Prayer: The Heart's True Home.* San Francisco: Harpers, 1992. ISBN: 978 0 06 053379-3.

- http://www.theworshipstudio.org/what-is-prophetic-art/

- http://www.newcreationfellowship.us/soaking.html

- www.soakingwithapurpose.com/soaking
- http://www.enddaysworship.com/Soaking%20Prayer.htmm
- https://slideplayer.com/slide/13494231/

www.ingramcontent.com/pod-product-compliance
Lightning Source LLC
Chambersburg PA
CBHW071154090426
42736CB00012B/2329